THINGS FOR KIDS TO DO

By Thelma Giffhorn

More than 100 learning activities to integrate with Bible stories!

Use this book with children at home or in group situations. Children may also use this book themselves.

VICTOR BOOKS a division of SP Publications, Inc.

WHEATON, ILLINOIS 60187

Offices also in
Whitby, Ontario, Canada
Amersham-on-the-Hill, Bucks, England

Second printing, 1985

Recommended Dewey Decimal Number: 372.5
Suggested Subject Headings: Arts and Crafts; Elementary
   Education; Manual Arts

Library of Congress Catalog Card Number: 84-52048

ISBN: 0-89693-525-6

VICTOR BOOKS
A division of SP Publications, Inc.
Wheaton, Illinois 60187

BIBLE STORIES
With Integrated Learning Experiences!

WHY this book?

It's no secret that children are active, learning people. They learn by doing: thinking, writing, drawing, painting, playing, creating—the list is endless.

This book guides their learning into meaningful activities that can be related to Bible stories and Bible truths.

Some activities are for early years; others for children in upper grades of elementary school. IF you are using the book at home, let the children choose activities with your guidance. IF you are using the book in a school, class, or group situation, give the children as much choice as possible, depending on materials and available guidance.

Children can handle many of the activities on their own. However, a helpful adult can make the activity a more effective learning experience.

WHAT'S in this book?

You will find condensations of five Bible stories about Peter. These stories easily correlate with the activities, but you can think of many more. For instance, a map can be used to make any Bible story come alive. Tabletop scenes, such as Jerusalem or the Sea of Galilee, relate to all biblical events taking place in these areas. Drawing pictures, writing a script, or making a living mural can all develop deeper understanding of biblical events.

One section contains easy-to-make recipes for paste, finger paint, clay, etc. Let your children enjoy making these low-cost materials.

You'll notice a code to indicate the difficulty of an activity. However, do not be limited by this. Many older children will enjoy some of the activities indicated for preschoolers. And some preschoolers will be able to do many of the crafts designated for elementary children.

ENJOY this book with children
—at home, at church, at camp, or school!

E	Going to the Temple	31
E	Gone Fishing	92
E	Guess What	81
P	Hanging Bird	112
P, E	How Seeds Grow	134
P, E	How to Preserve Leaves	135
P, E	Invitations	102
P	Jewish Coins	87
E	Kite	113
P, E	Leaf Imprint	114
E	Leather Bookmark	115
E	Living Mural	93
P, E	Magnetic Boats	43
P, E	Medallion	22
P, E	Melted Crayon	71
E	Multimedia Presentation	82
P, E	Mural	72
E	Musical Chairs	94
E	Net Full of Fish	51
E	News Broadcast	64

P	Night Scene Chalk Art	44
E	Oiled Design	116
P, E	Paint a Picture	73
E	Paint on Glass	95
P	Paint with Tempera	59
P, E	Papier-mâché Boat	23
E	Papier-mâché Fish	117
E	Paper Plate Bible Verses	65
P, E	Paper Plate Puppets	140
P	Pinecone Bird Feeder	118
P	Play Dough Bible Objects	74
E	Placemats	119
E	Pomander Ball	120
P	Poster Collage	75
P	Potato Printing	60
E	Punch Design	52
P	Puzzle	61
E	Questions and Answers	96

E	Radio Broadcast	32
E	Ring Toss	121
E	Road to Jerusalem	97
E	Rock Paperweights	33
E	Sand Candle	122
E	Sand Drawing	66
E	Sand Painting	123
P	Seashell Flowers	46
E	Seashell Paintings	98
E	Seed Mosaic	67
P, E	Sea of Galilee Scene	45
E	Soap Carving	34
P	Spatter Paint	24
E	Spice Swag	124
P, E	Sponge Garden	131
E	Stenciled Placemats	83
P, E	Stick Puppets	141
E	Story Cards	99
E	Story Pocket	84
P, E	String Art	125
P	Styrofoam Trays	76

P, E	Sunflower in a Carton	136
P, E	Sweet Potato Vine	133
E	Tape Recording	35
E	Terra Cotta Clay Tile	53
E	Tin Map of Israel	85
P	Tissue Overlay	25
P	Tissue Paper Flowers	126
E	Topographical Map	36
E	Tote Bag	100
E	TV Alert	54
E	Twelve Disciples	37
E	Walking in Peter's Shoes	68
E	Wall Hanging	127
E	Weather Story	55
P	Weaving	62
P	Whirly Bird	128
E	Wind Chimes	129
E	Wind Gauge	56
E	Yarn on Burlap	38

CONTENTS

Communicating God's Word
Bible stories by the Scripture Press Staff

Story 1 7
Peter Chooses to Follow Jesus
Story 2 9
Peter Learns Who Jesus Is
Story 3 11
Peter Denies Jesus
Story 4 13
Peter Hears the Good News
Story 5 15
Jesus Forgives Peter

Integrated Learning Experiences
Story 1 20-38
Story 2 39-56
Story 3 57-68
Story 4 69-85
Story 5 86-100

1, 2, 3, 4, 5 = Story Key: P = Preschool E = Elementary

5

Basic Recipes 17

Activities for Preschoolers

Story 1 20-25

Story 2 39-46

Story 3 57-62

Story 4 69-76

Story 5 86-87

SEE ALSO ALPHABETICAL INDEX 142

Activities for Older Children

Story 1 26-38

Story 2 47-56

Story 3 63-68

Story 4 77-85

Story 5 88-100

Bible Memorization Projects... 29, 51, 65, 77, 78, 92

Games to Play 31, 63, 68, 81, 91, 94, 96, 97

Publicity for Your Program 101

More Crafts 105

Growing Things 130

Puppets 137

1

PETER CHOOSES TO FOLLOW JESUS
Based on John 1:35-42; Luke 5:1-11

Andrew listened carefully to what his friend, John the Baptist, was saying. "One is coming after me who is more important than I am."

"Who can this be?" Andrew asked himself.

Suddenly John said, "Look! There's the One I'm talking about."

When Andrew heard these words, he followed the Man who was walking past. But following wasn't enough for Andrew. He wanted his brother to know Jesus too.

"Simon, Simon," Andrew shouted as he ran along the lakeshore toward Simon. It took time to persuade Simon to go with him, but Andrew succeeded and brought his brother to Jesus.

Jesus looked at Simon and said, "You are Simon, but from now on you'll be called Peter."

Peter and Andrew went back to their fishing, but one day they met Jesus again. They were washing their nets when they heard a murmuring sound—a crowd of people walking and talking.

Jesus called out, "Let Me use your boat, will you? Push it out from the shore so that the people can see and hear Me."

When Jesus finished preaching, He told Peter and Andrew to row out into deeper water. The two men had been fishing all day, but hadn't caught a single fish. Jesus told them to lower their nets for a catch of fish. Even though they couldn't understand what Jesus was asking, they obeyed. Imagine how surprised they were when the fish filled up the boat! In fact, the two men had to ask some other fishermen to help them pull in the net!

Jesus said to Peter, "Peter, don't be afraid because you have seen My power. Follow Me and you'll catch men—not merely fish."

"If any man serve Me, let him follow Me" (John 12:26).

2

PETER LEARNS WHO JESUS IS

Based on Luke 4:38-40; John 6:15-21; Matthew 14:22-33

Peter had decided to follow Jesus! And Peter saw Jesus do one of His early miracles in his own home.

As Jesus and Peter, with other friends, came into the house, Peter's wife may have said, "Peter, I'm so glad you're home. My mother is very sick. I don't know what to do for her."

Jesus went into the room and put His hand on the woman's head. Immediately she was well! Jesus had used His power to heal her!

Peter was sound asleep when Jesus got up very early the next morning to pray. Peter soon learned that Jesus often talked to His heavenly Father.

One evening Jesus was up in the hills praying. He had told His friends to get into a boat and go to the other side of the lake. They got into the boat and pushed off. It was evening and there was a strong breeze. The men rowed hard as they did their best to send the boat through the water.

Suddenly one man screamed, "What's that ahead?" Was it someone moving over the water?

Peter was the first to shout, "It's Jesus!" Jesus was walking on the water.

Then Peter cried out, "Lord, if it's really You, let me walk on the water too."

Jesus said, "Come on, Peter."

Immediately Peter stepped out of the boat and stood on the water. He took some steps, but then he took his eyes off Jesus. He was afraid! At that very moment, he started to sink. Jesus reached out and pulled Peter up. Together the two walked to the boat.

All of the men in the boat said, "Truly, You are the Son of God!"

"Love the Lord your God, and serve Him with all your heart and with all your soul" (Deuteronomy 11:13).

3

PETER DENIES JESUS
Based on Luke 22-23; Mark 14:26-31, 66-72

Peter could not seem to understand that Jesus had come to earth to die on the cross for the sins of the world.

One evening Jesus and His disciples were eating a special supper together. Again Jesus talked about dying on the cross. Peter said, "Lord, I am ready to go with You to prison and to death."

"Peter," said Jesus, "before the rooster crows twice tomorrow morning you will say three times that you don't even know Me!"

Peter could not believe what he was hearing. But Peter did say that he didn't know Jesus. Here's what happened.

Later that same evening, soldiers came to Jesus in an olive grove where He had gone to pray. They grabbed Jesus and took Him away. Peter was so frightened that he ran off in the darkness. Not one of the disciples stayed with Jesus.

The soldiers and Jewish leaders took Jesus to the Jewish Supreme Court. But the witnesses there couldn't agree in the things that they had to say against Jesus.

At first Peter had been very frightened. He had run away so that no one could arrest him. Then, as he thought it over, he must have decided to go to see what would happen to Jesus. He stayed outside the courtroom and warmed his hands over a charcoal fire. A servant girl came up to him and took a good look.

"Say," she said, "you were with that Man, Jesus."

"No," said Peter, "I don't even know what you're talking about."

Another girl saw Peter and said, "This man was with Jesus."

Again Peter said it wasn't so. Then another person standing near Peter said, "Surely you are one of His disciples."

"NO!" shouted Peter. "I never knew Him." Immediately the rooster crowed the second time. Then Peter remembered what Jesus had said.

"God . . . loved us, and sent His Son to be the propitiation for our sins" (1 John 4:10).

4

PETER HEARS THE GOOD NEWS

Based on John 20:1-19

"Jesus is dead!" That's what the disciples said, and they believed it. Jesus had been taken by the soldiers and condemned to death. He had died on the cross of Calvary. Perhaps they knew that Jesus' body had been taken down from the cross and buried in a tomb.

All of Jesus' friends were very sad. The One they loved and worshiped was dead!

Some of His friends, a group of women, wanted to take fragrant spices to His grave. This was the custom in Bible days.

Let's imagine that we're somewhere in Jerusalem with Peter and John. Suddenly the two men see Mary Magdalene running toward them.

"Peter, John," she calls out, "someone has taken Jesus' body from the tomb."

The two men don't believe her, so they run quickly to the tomb. John gets there first, but he waits for Peter. The two men see that the tomb is empty. They go back home feeling very sad.

In the meantime, Mary Magdalene goes back to the tomb. This time she sees two angels inside the tomb. They ask her why she is crying.

Mary tells them. Then she hears a voice near her say, "What are you crying about?"

"Oh," says Mary, "someone has taken away my Lord, and I don't know where to find Him. If you have taken Him, please tell me where you have put Him, and I'll get Him."

"Mary," said Jesus. Immediately Mary looked at Him. She had not recognized Jesus before. Now she knew who He was. She knew He was alive!

Later that evening, Jesus' friends were meeting behind locked doors because they were afraid for their lives. Suddenly, without opening the door, Jesus was inside the room with them. He spoke to them. They could all see that Jesus had come back to life. He was, and is the living Saviour!

"He is risen" (Mark 16:6).

14

5

JESUS FORGIVES PETER
Based on John 21

After the disciples realized that Jesus had come back to life, they returned to their homes near the Sea of Galilee. Jesus had told them that He would see them there (Matthew 28:10).

Peter and Andrew went back to fishing. One night, six of the other disciples went fishing with them.

It was a good night for fishing, but again and again the men pulled up an empty net. They tried a new spot, but the net was always empty. Finally, near morning, they decided to go ashore.

As they rowed toward land, they heard Someone call out, "Men, have you caught any fish?"

"No," some of them shouted back.

"Put your net on the other side of the boat," said the Man, "and you'll catch some fish."

The men lowered the net again, but on the right side of the boat. Immediately the net was heavy with fish.

15

Peter was the first one to realize that the Man was Jesus. He jumped out of the boat and waded to shore. There the Lord Jesus had built a fire and was broiling some fish. The men gathered around and ate together.

When breakfast was over, Jesus turned to Peter and asked, "Simon, do you love Me more than these others?"

"Yes," said Peter, "You know I love You like a friend."

"Feed My lambs," said Jesus. Then Jesus asked him the same question twice more: "Do you love Me?"

Peter hurt inside. Why was Jesus asking him three times about his love? "Lord," he said, "You know all things. You know that I love You."

Then Jesus said, "Follow Me!"

Now Peter knew that Jesus had forgiven him. He knew that Jesus wanted him to keep on following. Peter must have been happier than he had ever been in his whole life!

"If we confess our sin, He is faithful and just to forgive us our sin" (1 John 1:9).

Homemade Paste

2 cups salt
1 cup flour
¾ cup water

Mix salt, flour, and water.
Add more water for a stickier consistency.
Use to paste paper or fabric.

Baker's Play Dough

4 cups	flour
1 cup	salt
1½ cups	boiling water
1 T.	vegetable oil

Mix flour and salt in a bowl. Add vegetable oil and water slowly, stirring constantly.

When thickened, turn mixture onto floured board and knead. Roll with rolling pin and cut with cookie cutters.

Bake at 250 degrees 1 to 1½ hours. Paint with tempera paint. Dry and shellac.

Play Dough (No bake)

4 cups	flour
2 cups	salt
2 cups	water
2 T.	vegetable oil
Few drops of food coloring	
4 tsp.	cream of tartar

Mix flour, salt, and cream of tartar. In a separate container add food coloring and oil to water. Add liquid to flour and salt mixture.

Cook over low heat till very stiff.

Knead on floured surface.

After using, play dough may be stored in a plastic container or Ziploc bag. Refrigerate.

Clay Dough

1 cup	cornstarch
2 cups	baking soda
1½ cups	cold water

Combine cornstarch and baking soda in a medium-size pan. Add water. Cook over medium heat, stirring constantly.

When mixture thickens, remove from heat. When cool, turn out on smooth surface covered with cornstarch. Knead.

Shape to desired form. Let dry for several days.

Paint with tempera. When dry, shellac.

Finger Paint

1 cup	laundry starch
1 cup	cold water
4 cups	boiling water
1 cup	Ivory Snow

Few drops of food coloring or tempera paint

Mix starch in cold water. Add boiling water to starch solution. Cook on stove till clear, stirring constantly. Add soap. Remove from stove and cool.

Add food coloring or tempera. Add a few drops of oil of cinnamon or peppermint, if you like. Store in refrigerator till ready to use on the smooth side of shelf or other similar paper.

If you prefer, follow a quick method to make finger paint by adding a few drops of food coloring or tempera paint to liquid starch.

INTEGRATED
ACTIVITIES

1-P
Collage

Gather some objects of different textures found by the sea. Glue onto a box, wood, metal, or posterboard.

Suggested materials:

grass corks stones cord yarn shells
seaweed feathers sand seeds string driftwood

Adapt activities to other Bible stories!

This activity, as well as others on following pages, correlates with any story about the Sea of Galilee.

Musht Fish

Fish Mosaic

Cut shape of fish from poster board. Tear pieces of construction paper. Glue on fish for scales. Use felt marker to draw details on fins and tail.

This is the type of fish Peter caught when Jesus told him to cast his net in the Sea of Galilee. Peter obeyed and caught the fish with the shekel in its mouth used for the tax money. The musht is found in abundance in the Sea of Galilee.

Medallion

Roll self-hardening clay ¼″ thick.

Cut a circle with cookie cutter or knife, making a 3″ disc. Draw design with nail. Also use nail to make initial on back. Make large hole in top with nail.

When dry, insert 6″ piece of yarn or string through hole. Then attach a leather strip or yarn to make a necklace. If "necklace" is attached directly to medallion, it will not hang straight.

You may adapt all of these activities for other Bible stories.

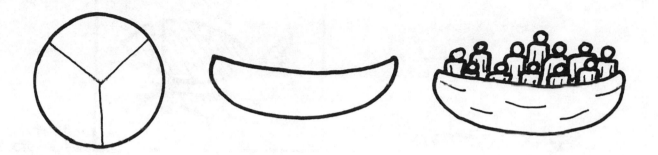

Papier-mâché Boat

Cut large styrofoam ball in thirds. Tape plastic wrap around section of ball.

Cut 1″ strips of newspaper. Make wallpaper paste according to directions on package. Dip strips of paper in paste. Place on styrofoam form. Cover with several thicknesses.

When dry, remove from form and paint with brown tempera paint. Shellac. Fill with chenille wire figures of disciples and Jesus.

Cut away
shaded areas.

Spatter Paint

2 cups tempera
2 cups water
Work in a cardboard carton to protect working area.

Cut a design on typing paper. You will spatter paint around this design.

Cut a 6″ square of wire screening. Place design on construction paper. Mix tempera in a bowl. Dip toothbrush in tempera. Hold screen above construction paper. Rub toothbrush across screen to spatter paint. Remove design.

You may use white shoe polish on colored construction paper for the same effect.

Star of David
Cut two triangles.

Tissue Overlay

Tear strips of colored tissue paper and dip in a bowl filled with
diluted white glue. Place the strips of tissue paper on waxed paper,
overlapping the edges. Allow to dry.

Make a frame of the desired shape from black construction paper.
Glue the frame to the dry tissue. Trim any tissue that protrudes
over edges. This gives a stained-glass effect when placed on a
window.

Another activity is to bend a coat hanger in a free-form shape.
Cover with coats of tissue paper dipped in glue.

1-E

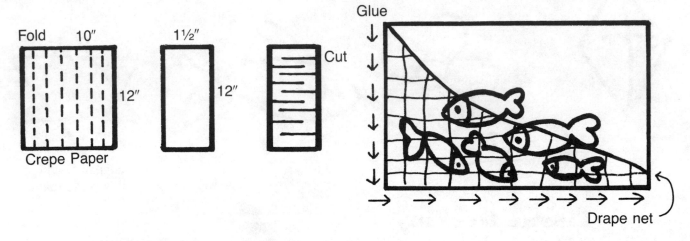

Cast Net Collage

Cut crepe paper 12″ x 10″.

Fold to measure 12″ x 1½″.

Cut paper 1″ deep every 1½″ along the 12″ side.

Pull net apart. Glue or tape to one side and drape across the bottom of 9″ x 12″ blue construction paper.

Pull loose edge of net to corner of paper. Glue.

Cut fish from construction paper. Fill net.

The Big Fisherman

Designer T-shirt

Make a design on stencil paper or poster board. Cut away the shaded area.

Place T-shirt on fabric hoop or pad of newspaper. Tape and pin shirt and stencil in place. Point heads of pins toward the inside of the design.

Dip round stiff stencil brush in fabric paint. Wipe off excess paint on paper towel. Brush over stencil in circular motion, away from edge of stencil toward center of open space on fabric. Use a different brush for each color. Use black ball-point fabric paint tube for writing.

Stenciling can be done on tennis shoes, burlap, denim, brown paper bags, and other materials.

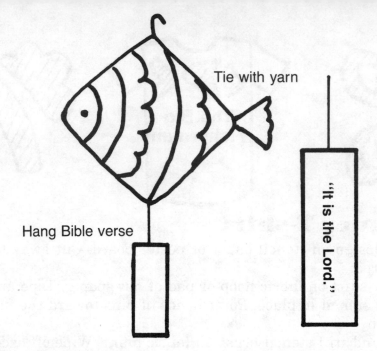

Tie with yarn

Hang Bible verse

"It is the Lord."

Fish

Bend a coat hanger to make a fish shape. Stretch nylon hose over hanger.

Cut decorative strips of construction paper. Fasten inside hose with dots of glue. To make tail, tie hose with yarn and clip.

Write a Bible verse on a strip of poster board. Hang from fish with string. Hang fish from ceiling.

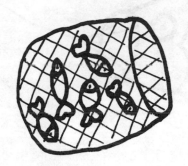
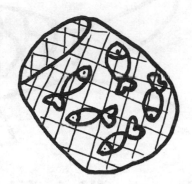

Fish in Nets

Save net bags from produce—oranges, onions, potatoes. Make fish from colored construction paper.

Write a Bible verse for each favorite Bible story on strip of white paper. Glue on top of fish.

Place fish in net. Draw a fish and tell the Bible story.

Flying Fish Kite

On two 12" x 36" sheets of butcher paper, draw a fish shape. Place two sheets together, cutting the two fish at the same time.

Use fiber-tip pens or crayons to decorate both sides exactly the same. Glue together around edge, leaving an opening at each end.

Make a wire hoop to fit the mouth. Tape hoop to mouth, reinforcing entire mouth with masking tape.

Tie four strings to mouth as shown. If available, fasten to a fishing snap swivel. Tie long string to fly kite.

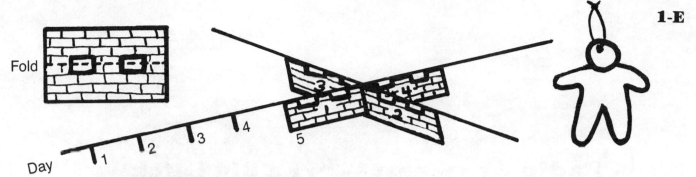

Fold

Day 1 2 3 4 5

Going to the Temple

Stretch two wires across the room, crossing at the center. Divide your group into four teams.

Fold four 12″ x 18″ sheets construction paper. With fiber-tip pens or crayons make the temple walls to look like blocks of marble. Use a different color for each team.

Fasten to center of wires, giving each team a section of wire.

Cut a construction paper person for each child, writing name of child on it. When a child is present, move his figure to next section of wire.

On last day, all children present arrive at the temple. Give one point for each figure at the temple. The team with the most points wins.

Radio Broadcast — "The Big Catch"

Script
Sound Effects
Mikes
Cast
Tape Recorder

1. Write the script.
2. Choose: announcer, director of production, sound effects person, cast.
3. Record sound effects on tape.
4. Rehearse.
5. Perform.
6. What do you want people to remember from the broadcast?

Rock Paperweights

Choose smooth rocks of various sizes and shapes.

Put a dab of glue on the area where you wish to stick another rock. Allow glue to dry.

Reapply glue and add second rock or rocks.

After the glue sets, use paint for detail.

"The Lord is my rock, and my fortress, and my deliverer; my God, my strength, in whom I will trust" (Psalm 18:2).

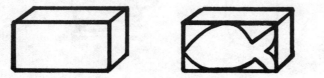

Soap Carving

Choose a bar of white soap.
Outline a shape on both sides with a pencil.
Use a small kitchen knife for carving.

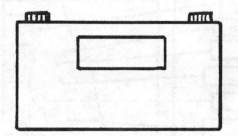

Tape Recording (Peter Meets Jesus)

Make a tape recording of the Bible story. Play it back as the children engage in various Bible-related activities. Give any volunteers an opportunity to tape the Bible story and listen to their own voices as they play it back.

You may wish to pre-record the Bible story and play it for someone in a nursing home. The children involved could wear costumes and pantomime the story.

"That which we have seen and heard declare we unto you" (1 John 1:3).

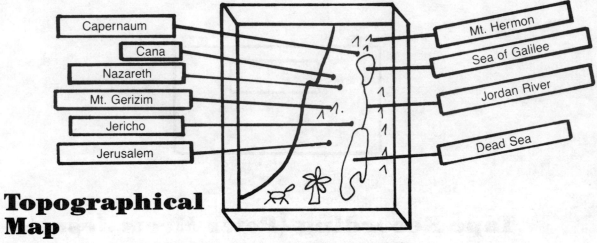

Capernaum
Cana
Nazareth
Mt. Gerizim
Jericho
Jerusalem

Mt. Hermon
Sea of Galilee
Jordan River
Dead Sea

Topographical Map

Find or draw a map of Israel, approximately 15″ x 36″.

Place map on sheet of plywood. Make a 2″ edge with strips of wood molding. Cover mountainous areas with small pieces of window screen shaped like mountains. Tack to board.

Mix plaster of paris. When thick, pour over map with the exception of lakes, seas, and rivers.

When dry, paint with tempera paint. Paint small pieces of sponge green for trees. Make houses and buildings with small blocks of wood. Make people and animals with chenille wire.

Twelve Disciples

Fold three sheets of paper four times. Draw the paper figure.

Cut around the edge, except where hands are joined.

Open papers and tape to make chain of figures.

Help children write names of 12 disciples: Matthew, James, John, Thomas, Peter, Andrew, Simon, James the less, Judas, Philip, Nathanael, and Bartholomew.

Yarn on Burlap

Cut burlap in pieces 14″ x 20″.

Fringe edges for placemats.

Draw pencil design of a Bible story on burlap. Outline the design with glue.

Place colored yarn on the glue. For variation, sew yarn instead of using glue.

Invite a friend to help make the placemats. Tell the Bible story as you use the mats for lunch. Let your friend take a mat home and tell the Bible story to his/her family.

All of these activities may be adapted for other Bible stories!

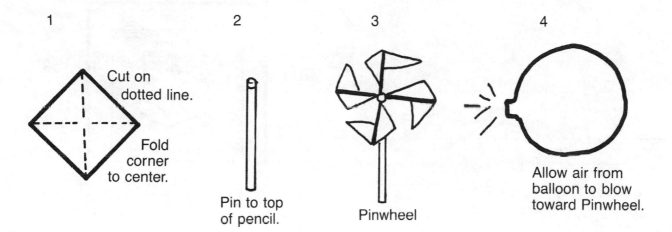

1
Cut on dotted line.

Fold corner to center.

2
Pin to top of pencil.

3
Pinwheel

4
Allow air from balloon to blow toward Pinwheel.

Air Power

Make a pinwheel from stiff paper according to illustrations. Inflate a balloon. Release air from the balloon in the direction of the pinwheel. What happens?

God cares for you.

Crayon Rubbings

Place a cardboard shape under a piece of typing paper. Color over the paper with crayon. Mount crayon rubbing on construction paper. Write a title at the bottom of the page.

You may make outdoor rubbings by placing the paper on a tree, concrete walk, or a brick wall. Rub with crayon to illustrate various textures.

Andrew

Jesus

Peter

John

James

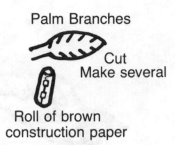

Palm Branches

Cut
Make several

Roll of brown
construction paper

Diorama of Capernaum

Choose a small box or empty shoe box. Glue light blue construction paper to inside of box for sky. The wall around the city may be made from construction paper. Use tan paper for ground.

Glue construction paper around match boxes, spice cans, or gelatin boxes for buildings.

Palm trees may be made from green construction-paper leaves taped to a brown construction-paper trunk. Chenille wires may be used to make figures. Stand people and trees in plasticine or florist's clay.

Gifts from God's Wonders

Choose dry materials—pebbles or seashells. Let the child use plasticine or florist's clay to fasten materials to driftwood, rock, or boards.

Talk about the Sea of Galilee where Peter walked, the various uses for trees, plants, etc.

This makes a thoughtful gift.

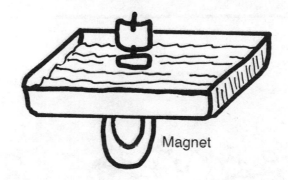

Magnet

Magnetic Boats

Provide each child with one-half cork cut lengthwise, thumbtack, toothpick, construction-paper scraps, and scissors. Several children may share aluminum cake pan filled with water. Provide a magnet for each child.

Place the thumbtack in the bottom of the half cork. Press the toothpick into the top. Make a small sail and place on toothpick. Depending on the size of cork, break a toothpick in half.

Place the boat in the water. Hold the cake pan or support it in some way so that the magnet may be moved under it. As magnet is moved, boat will "sail."

Night Scene Chalk Art

Choose dark blue or black construction paper for background of a
night scene. Use white or yellow chalk. Glue cotton balls for moon.
Pull some to shape and use for foam on waves.

Sea of Galilee

Sea of Galilee Scene

Cut a piece of shelf paper or white plastic to fit the tabletop. Use indelible markers to draw Sea of Galilee. Paint sea with blue tempera, finger paint, or crayon.

Make papier-mâché boats and chenille-wire people.

Make nets from hair nets and fill with construction-paper fish.

45

Seashell Flowers

Glue a group of seashells in the shape of a flower on construction
paper, a wooden board, or wooden box. Use chenille wire for stems.

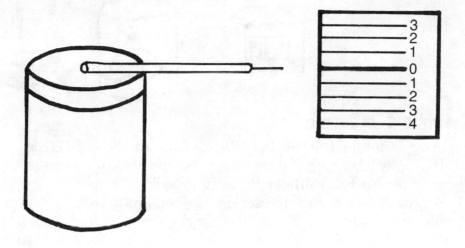

Barometer

You will need a 1-pound or 2-pound empty coffee can.

Place the plastic lid on top of the can. Tape a needle to the end of a straw. Fasten the straw securely to the top of the lid.

Make a chart as shown above with each line ¼ centimeter apart. Place the barometer as close as possible to the chart with the needle at the "0". Observe changes in weather.

Boats Galore

Prepare a label for the display: "Boats from the Sea of Galilee." Children may also make a list of events that took place on or near the sea. Consult the Bible or Bible storybook.

1. Scraps of Wood: Provide scraps of wood and nails.

2. Walnut Shell Boat: Place florist's clay inside walnut shell. Cut sail from construction paper and insert toothpick. Push sail into the florist's clay.

3. Aluminum Potato Boat: Purchase aluminum potato shells from the grocery store. Make sail from scraps of fabric or construction paper. Cut slits in the sail for a popsicle stick mast. Stand mast in florist's clay or plasticene clay.

4. Provide additional materials for children to create other Bible-time boats.

Decorate other object with boats. Secure an empty carton from an ice cream store. Trim with burlap, felt, and yarn.

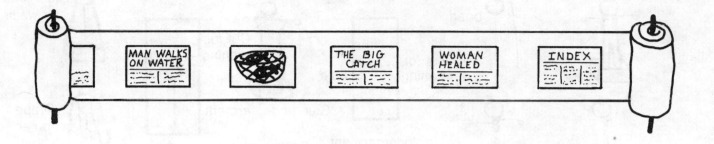

Capernaum News

Write a newspaper. Include: front page index, editorial, feature article, news release, illustrations, fashions, cartoons, society news, letters to the editor, sports, advertising, classified ads, and "the Scroll Review."

Assign sections or let volunteers choose. Glue each article on a shelf-paper scroll. Start at the right and work toward left, following Jewish style. Glue ends of scroll on wood dowels.

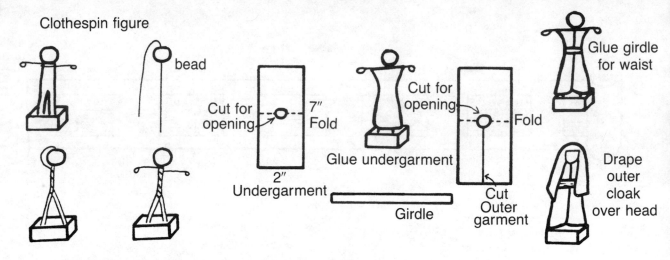

Clothespin figure

bead

Cut for opening 7" Fold

2" Undergarment

Cut for opening

Glue undergarment

Girdle

Fold

Cut Outer garment

Glue girdle for waist

Drape outer cloak over head

Clothespin or Chenille Wire Figures

1. Clothespin Figure: Stand clothespin in 2" square of styrofoam. Cut 6" chenille wire. Twist around neck for arms. Make face with fiber-tip marker.

2. Chenille Wire Figure: Stick 12" wire through bead for head. Twist for body. Stand legs in 2" square styrofoam. Cut 6" wire. Twist around neck for arms. Make face on bead with fiber-tip marker.

3. Cut and glue fabric. Use yarn for hair and men's beards.

Net Full of Fish

Cut fish from construction paper.

Write Bible reference on fish. Place in net, made from a net bag.

Two players or teams play. Player from first team draws fish from net and reads reference. If player says verse correctly, he keeps fish. If not word perfect, fish goes back in net.

Other team takes a turn. Team with most fish at end of game wins.

Punch Design

Show a finished punch design. Have children draw their own patterns on typing paper.

Place several thicknesses of magazines or newspaper over the work area. Tape pattern to 8″ x 10″ sheet of tin or copper foil. (May purchase these materials from a metal shop.)

Gently tap outline with hammer and nail to make design.

Mount on a pre-stained board with 20-gauge ½″ nails, or fasten to an 8″ x 10″ frame with a thin line of clear silicone rubber caulking.

Clean with steel wool and spray with clear lacquer.

Terra Cotta Clay Tile

Roll self-hardening clay with a rolling pin.

Use small knife to trim to desired size.

Carefully arrange seashells to make a design. Cover with waxed paper to hold design in place. Gently roll over design with rolling pin. Remove waxed paper.

Make two holes in center top for hanging. Hang with yarn, ribbon, or strip of leather.

TV Alert

Make a weather poster to use on television as a warning for inclement weather. Use tempera paint, tissue overlay, finger paint, fiber-tip markers, or crayon. Feature a Bible event.

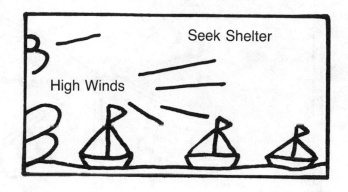

Weather Story

Write a story about a wind storm on a lake, a hurricane, an earthquake, a tornado, or a blizzard.

Illustrate with tempera paint, tissue overlay, a collage, or a mural.

Talk about God's power and protection.

Adapt these activities to a variety of Bible stories.

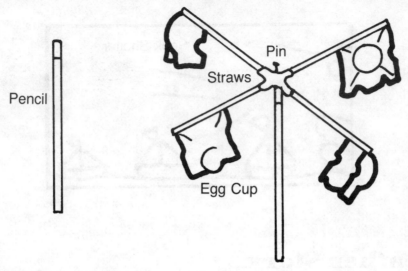

Wind Gauge

Tape two straws together at center. Pin straws on top of a pencil.

Cut four cups from an egg carton. Tape to ends of straws. Mark the counter cup with a fiber-tip pen.

Hold gauge outdoors in a gentle breeze. Count the number of turns it makes in a minute. Divide this by 10. This will give you the approximate wind speed. A wind gauge is called an *anemometer*.

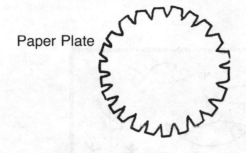

Paper Plate

Baskets

On a 12″ paper plate cut an uneven number of slits 2″ deep. Widen each slit at the top.

Cut 12″ strips of crepe paper. Twist crepe paper. Weave strips of crepe paper in and out, shaping basket. Glue beginning and end of each strip.

When the entire area is covered, glue last strip around top.

Apply protective coat of shellac.

Fill with grain, if available.

Baskets were made primarily of cane during Bible times. They were used to carry food. The baskets used to carry grain for tithes were not used for any other purpose.

"Blessed shall be thy basket and thy store" (Deuteronomy 28:5).

Crayon Resist

½ cup tempera

2 cups water

With crayons, draw a design or picture on construction paper. Press firmly so crayoned areas have a heavy waxed surface.

After the picture is completed, brush the entire area with the thin tempera paint solution.

Write the Bible verse or the name of the story on a separate paper and staple to the picture.

Paint with Tempera

    1 cup powdered tempera (purchased at art stores)
    2 cups water
    2 cups detergent

Mix the three ingredients to make paint. Store in plastic container with lid. Use a separate container for each color. Start with two or three colors: red, yellow, blue; then add green, brown, and others. Place several containers in a plastic shoe box for storage. Use an art brush 1″ wide for each color.

    Have the child paint a picture of the Bible story or verse on large newsprint. After he/she has completed a picture, write the name of the Bible story across the bottom of the picture. Perhaps the child will ask you to write a sentence from the Bible story or the Bible verse.

Cut away.

Leave design

Shelf Paper

Potato Printing

2 cups powdered tempera
2 cups water
1 potato

Mix tempera, purchased at art store, with water. Place in shallow pan. Cut desired shape from end of potato and dip in paint mixture.

Stamp on colored construction paper for greeting cards. Make gift wrapping paper by stamping design on shelf paper.

You may choose to use a cookie cutter, potato masher, or other gadgets for printing instead of the potato.

Puzzle

Make picture on poster board with felt-tip marker. Work on several pads of newspaper.

Use an Exacto knife to cut shapes of puzzle. Place in plastic bag to store.

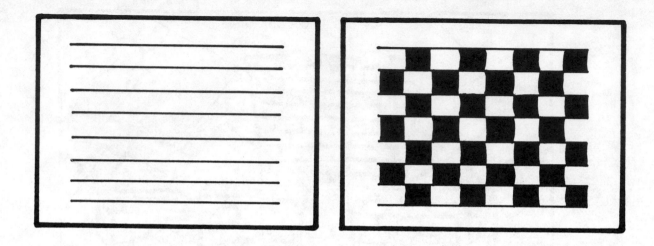

Weaving

Choose an 18″ x 12″ piece of construction paper. Cut slits 1″ apart the length of the paper. Leave 1″ on all sides.

Cut different colored 1″ strips of construction paper to weave mat. Glue each strip at the end.

The women in Israel wove the fabric for their clothing on looms.

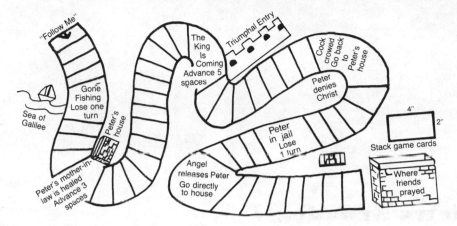

Bibleland Game

Make a series of game cards 2" x 4". Write a question on each card about the life of Peter.

Also on each card, write the number 1, 2, or 3. This is the number of spaces the player advances if he answers the question correctly.

Make a master sheet with questions and answers to check players.

Draw a gameboard on 22" x 28" poster board, or other suitable material. The illustration is based on Peter's life. Design your board for Bible coverage appropriate to your group.

You may adapt all of these activities for other Bible stories.

News Broadcast

Here are some suggestions for your radio news program:

WVBS Evening News

Presents the report on today's happenings in Jerusalem, including: Jesus' arrest, Peter's denial, Jesus' death.

Interviews with: some of Jesus' disciples, Peter, the girl who questioned Peter.

"We cover the news behind the news! We tell you not just the facts, but how people felt about the facts. How did Jesus' disciples feel when He was arrested? What did they do? How did Peter feel? What did Peter do that made him ashamed? How did Jesus' followers feel about His death?"

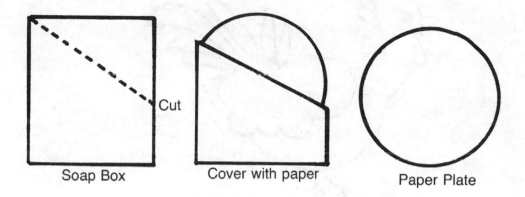

Soap Box — Cut

Cover with paper

Paper Plate

Paper Plate Bible Verses

Write Bible verses on paper plates. Decorate edges with fiber-tip markers. Put reference on back of each plate.

Cut a laundry detergent box as shown. Cover box with self-adhesive paper. Store paper plates in box.

Sand Drawing

Protect working area with newspaper.

Make a design on dark blue or black construction paper. Outline design with white glue. Before it dries, sprinkle sand on glue. Tap excess sand from paper.

Seed Mosaics

Cut a shape from cardboard. Choose seeds of various sizes, shapes, and colors. Glue to cardboard to form pattern. Place hook on back. Hang on wall.

Substitute any of these for seeds: small pebbles, various sizes and shapes of macaroni, pasta, small squares cut or torn from construction paper, or paper confetti.

Walking in Peter's Shoes

Draw around foot on construction paper. Cut out.

Write Bible verse on one side. Write Bible reference on reverse side of foot. Place footprints across floor with reference on top.

Game may be played by two or more players or by two teams. First player stands on first footprint. He must say the verse word-perfect before advancing to the next footprint. Turn footprint over, read verse aloud to check for accuracy.

Player keeps footprint if he has repeated verse accurately. Player or team with most footprints wins.

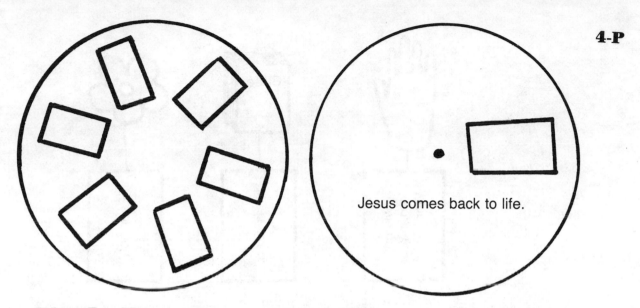

Jesus comes back to life.

Circle Board

Make a sequence of pictures. Glue them on a large poster board circle.

Cut a second circle the same size. Make a window large enough to show a picture.

Fasten two circles at center with brad paper fastener. Turn outer circle to tell story.

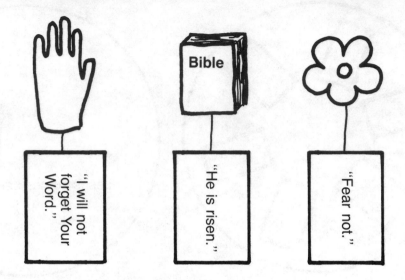

Crepe Paper Relief

Protect working area with newspaper before starting project.

Cut desired shape from poster board. Tear bits of crepe paper. Add to a mix of wallpaper paste and water. Mix to a creamy consistency.

Apply to design with wooden tongue depressor or spatula.

When dry, write Bible verse on a strip of poster board. Hang from shape with nylon fishing line. Hang crepe paper relief from ceiling.

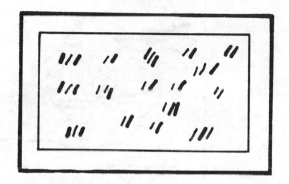

Melted Crayon

Place crayon shavings between two sheets of waxed paper. Iron together with warm iron. Mount and hang in window. Protect the ironing board with several sheets of newspaper. Also, place newspaper on top of the waxed paper while ironing.

You may adapt all of these activities for other Bible stories.

"Cast your nets on the other side."

Mural

Provide a large roll of shelf paper and a box of crayons. After reading a favorite Bible story the child may wish to make a pictorial account of the events.

After the sequence of pictures is completed, you or the child may write about each event. The name of the story or Bible verse should be written across the top of the mural.

Instead of using crayons, use tempera paint, fiber-tip markers, or make figures and objects from construction paper, chenille wire, netting, and other objects. Glue on mural.

"He careth for you."

Paint a Picture

Choose a large sheet of newsprint. Leave a space at the bottom to write a sentence about the Bible story or a memory verse.

Provide tempera paint. Children may use 1″ and larger brushes, or you may fasten 2″ pieces of sponge to clamp-type clothespins.

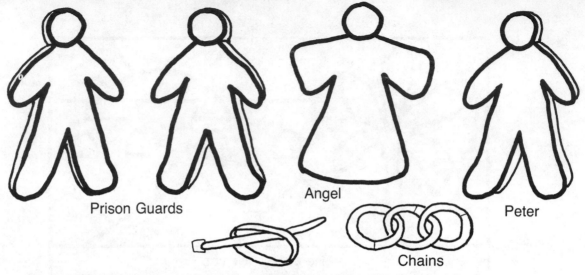

Prison Guards

Angel

Peter

Chains

Play Dough Bible Objects

4 cups flour   1½ cup boiling water

1 cup salt   1 T vegetable oil

Mix flour and salt in a bowl. Add vegetable oil and water slowly, stirring constantly.

When thickened, turn mixture onto floured board and knead. Roll with rolling pin and cut with cookie cutters or mold with hands.

Bake at 250° for 1 to 1½ hours.

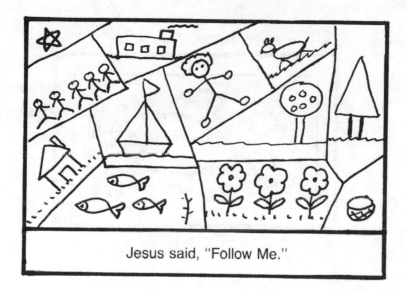

Jesus said, "Follow Me."

Poster Collage

Draw pictures or cut from magazines. Glue all on a large piece of poster board. Overlap edges of some pictures; glue at various angles.

Write the Bible verse across the bottom. This makes a meaningful wall decoration for a child's room.

Styrofoam Trays

Save styrofoam trays used for meat and produce.

Outline with glue a design or scene on the tray to illustrate a Bible story.

Place yarn, fabric, and small objects on glued surface to complete the picture.

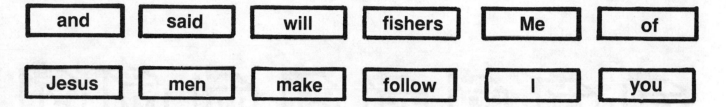

Bible Verse Scramble

Write a Bible verse on 3″ x 5″ cards, one word on each card. Code each word card of the verse with the same color. Mix up the words. Stack in a pile and secure with a rubber band.

Do seven more verses the same way, but with a different color to code each verse.

Make at least ten sets of these eight verses.

Give a set of the eight verses to each player.

A caller states the color of the verse to be unscrambled. The first person finished stands. Wait until each person has unscrambled his words. Then person standing reads verse.

Scramble words again and put them back in the rubber band. Person in charge calls next color. Proceed until all verses are read.

Bible Verse Village

Choose wood scraps for small blocks.

Paint blocks with white or pastel acrylic paint. Draw windows and doors in black. Write short Bible verse or phrase, one letter for each block.

This makes a nice gift to be displayed on a shelf or desk.

City of Jerusalem

Choose a large cardboard box for the base of the city. Cut sides of box, leaving 6″ to 8″ to form wall around city.

Make a thin solution of white glue. Brush on bottom of box. Quickly sprinkle a thin layer of sand.

Cut small blocks of wood from scrap lumber for houses. Paint buildings and wall with white or gray acrylic paint. When dry, paint with black outline to give appearance of stone. The temple was white marble.

Make palm trees with construction paper, and figures from chenille wire.

Gifts from God's Creation

Choose dry materials, pebbles, feathers, dried flowers, seeds, seashells, or other nature objects. Glue materials to driftwood, rock, or boards. You may also use florist's tape or plasticine.

Talk about God's creation and the various uses for trees, plants, etc.

Tape on an appropriate Bible verse, such as Psalm 8:1.

This makes a thoughtful gift.

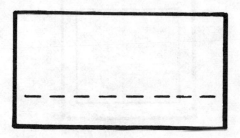

Guess What

Divide into two teams. Leader of first team chooses a word from a Bible character's life, and whispers it to someone not playing. This person draws a blank for each letter of the word. Use chalkboard or large sheet of paper.

The other team chooses a letter, but not a vowel.

If letter is in word, leader of the first team writes this letter in the blank. Anyone on the team may choose a letter.

When a member of the team is ready to guess the word, he must tell the leader of the team. Only the leader may say the word. When one team guesses the word the other team takes a turn.

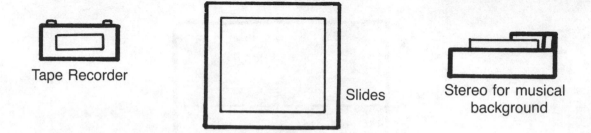

Tape Recorder

Slides

Stereo for musical background

Multimedia Presentation

Choose a travel brochure or a scenic postcard picture of Israel. (The picture must have a clay base.) Cut picture to be a 2″ square.

Cut a 2″ square of transparent Con-Tact paper. Peel off protective cover. Place sticky side down on picture. Soak in soapy water for about 30 minutes. Peel Con-Tact paper from picture. Image will adhere to self-adhesive paper. Dry with paper towel.

Mount on 35mm transparency slide mount purchased from camera shop.

Another method uses blank transparencies (slides). Draw pictures with markers to illustrate the Bible story.

Write Bible narrative. Make tape recording using Hebrew music for background.

Stenciled Placemats

Draw a design on stencil paper or poster board. Cut away shaded areas.

Hem white cotton fabric or fringe burlap 20″ x 14″ for placemat.

Place fabric on hoop or pad of newspaper. Tape in place. Pin stencil to fabric. Place heads of pins toward the inside of design.

Dip round stiff stencil brush in fabric paint. Wipe off excess paint on paper towel. Brush in circular motion away from edge of stencil toward center of open space on fabric. Use different brush for each color.

The same procedure may be used to make a design on a wooden basket, piece of wood, or construction paper.

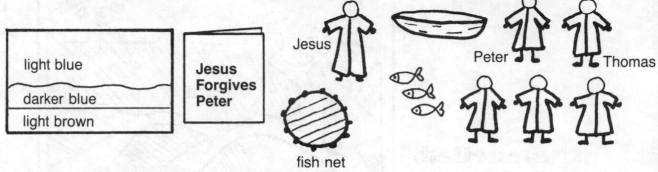

light blue

darker blue

light brown

Jesus
Forgives
Peter

Jesus

fish net

Peter

Thomas

Story Pocket

Glue a backing of light blue construction paper on a manila folder. Cut a strip of darker blue and tape across the lower middle of the page for water. Tape the bottom and sides on the folder to form pocket.

Cut a strip of light brown for the seashore. Tape to bottom edge of folder, forming another pocket.

Cut people and props from 3″ x 5″ cards.

Decorate with scraps of fabric, yarn, netting, or construction paper. Use fiber-tip pens for detail. Store small pieces in plastic bag. Clip to folder.

Write name of story on folder.

Tin Map of Israel

Place several thicknesses of magazines or newspapers on board or work area. Tape a map of Israel on a sheet of tin or copper foil, or on lid of a large tin can.

Ahead of time, stain a piece of plywood for a mount. When map is completed, nail to plywood with 20 gauge ½″ nails.

Gently tap outline of map through tin with hammer and nail.

Instead of using tin, this activity may be done by taping map to construction paper and poking holes around outline of map with a pin.

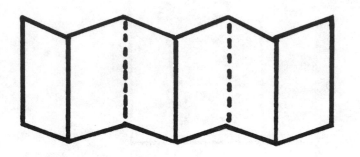

Lame
Man
Healed

Folding Book

Cut construction paper in strips 18″ x 4″. Make accordion folds as illustrated.

Pages measure 3″ x 4″. Make cover of book. Number each page.

By drawing and writing show the sequence of events in a Bible story, such as healing of the lame man at the Beautiful Gate (Acts 3:1-10).

You may adapt all of these activities for other Bible stories.

Shekel   Half Shekel

Jewish Coins

Make a circle of self-hardening clay about ¼" thick. Inscribe the insignia of the shekel and half shekel on the clay with the sharp point of a nail.

You may also make coins from construction paper with crayons or fiber-tip markers.

The shekel was a Jewish coin. Each Jew over 20 was required to bring a half shekel to the temple each year as well as one tenth of his crops. Money changers, who sat behind little wooden tables in the temple, became wealthy by cheating the poor.

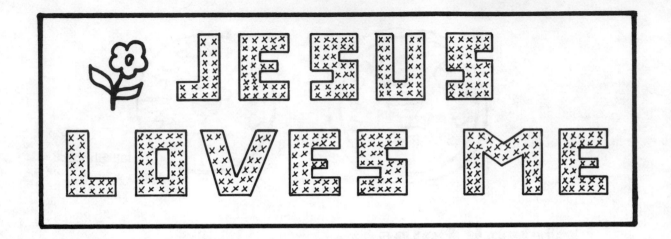

Cross-stitch

Cut an 8½″ x 10½″ piece of fabric for cross-stitch.

Sketch pattern on fabric with blue dressmaker's pencil.

Decide on a color scheme. Use a single strand of embroidery floss for cross-stitch.

When finished, rub off markings with a damp cloth. Frame in an 8″ x 10″ frame.

Felt Board

On manila folder, glue a background of blue felt for sky. Cut strips of tan and brown felt for hills and foreground. Cut strips of green felt for grass. These will adhere to felt or flannel background.

Shapes for the sun, moon and stars, people, animals, and trees may also be cut from felt.

Place objects on the felt board as you tell the Bible story.

Store scenery and small pieces in plastic bag. Place inside folder.

Make a separate folder for each Bible story.

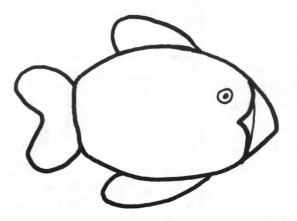

Fish Cushion

Cut shape of large fish from 24 sheets of newspaper. Staple around edges, leaving a small opening.

Stuff with wads of paper—newspaper or tissue. Staple shut.

Paint with tempera paint. When dry, shellac.

This is a decorative pillow. Do not sit on it or shellac may come off on clothing.

Fish Game

Cut fish from poster board. Place a paper clip over the end of each fish.

Tie a string to end of a dowel stick. Tie a magnet to the other end.

Write a question about Peter's life on each fish. Write the answer on the reverse side. Scatter the fish, question side up.

If the player who catches a fish can answer the question correctly, he may catch another fish and continue playing until he misses. Proceed to the next player.

Player with the most fish at the end of a game wins. Store fish and pole in a manila envelope.

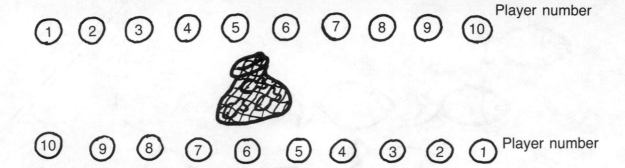

Gone Fishing (Bible Memorization)

Write Bible verses on construction-paper fish. Write the Bible references on opposite sides of the fish.

Place fish in net at center of room. Choose two teams.

Line up teams facing each other with the net in the center.

Caller stands on net. He draws a fish from the net; reads the references; then places it on top of the net.

When fish touches the net, players #1 may run for the fish. The first one to pick up the fish may say the verse.

If the verse is said "word perfect," player takes fish. If player misses, return fish to net and caller draws another fish.

When all fish are out of net, team with most fish at given time wins.

Living Mural

Make a mural for a variety of Bible stories. Use freezer paper or oilcloth. For the story of the healing of the lame man (Acts 3:1-11), for example, draw Herod's temple and the Beautiful Gate with fiber-tip markers.

Cut out circles on mural the size of a child's head. You may put masking tape around holes.

Write a script to go with the story.

Children take the parts and speak with faces showing through cut-out circles on mural.

I lived at Peter's house.
Jesus healed me.
Who am I?

Musical Chairs

Write questions about Peter on 3″ x 5″ cards. Describe a person, place, or event. Write the answers on the reverse sides. Have same number of chairs as players.

Place cards on chairs, question side showing. Start the music. When music stops each player sits on chair closest to him.

Start with first chair. Player stands and reads question. When he answers question, turn the card over to check answer. If he misses, he is out of game. Move to second player. After each person has had a turn, start music and continue game. (Do not remove a chair). Set a time limit on this game.

Paint on Glass

Paint the outline of a picture with black acrylic paint. Fill in detail with appropriate colors.

When paint is dry, trim edge with colored plastic tape. Make loop at center to hang in window.

> I lived at Peter's House.
> Jesus healed me.
> Who am I?

Questions and Answers

On 3″ x 5″ cards, write questions about places, people, and events in Peter's life. Write answers on the reverse side.

Choose a caller to read the questions. The first person who thinks he knows the answer stands. If player answers correctly, he gets the card. Player with the most cards wins.

Store game in manila folder. Write the name of the game on the front of the folder.

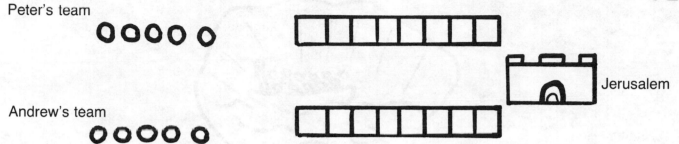

Peter's team

Andrew's team

Jerusalem

Road to Jerusalem

Make as many as 10-15 squares on shelf paper for each team.

Write questions on 3″ x 5″ cards with answers on reverse side. Choose two teams. Have a caller read questions.

Caller reads question to first player on Peter's team. If he answers correctly, he goes to square one.

Andrew's team is next. If player misses the next question, it is given to Peter's team.

The first team to reach Jerusalem wins.

Store game in manila folder with name of game on folder.

Seashell Paintings

Find large, flat shells. Clean thoroughly.

Paint a picture of the Sea of Galilee with acrylic paint.

Write a Bible verse with #00 paint brush. You may type Bible verse on strip of paper and glue to shell.

When dry, spray with a fixative shellac. Makes an excellent gift for a sick person or friend.

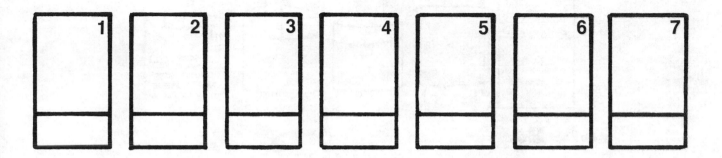

Story Cards

Tell a Bible story.

Provide material to make a series of pictures about a Bible story.

Typing paper may be used with pencil sketches or crayon. Number the pictures.

Spread the pictures on the floor. Ask volunteers to retell the story with the illustrations. This teaches sequencing of ideas and reinforces concepts.

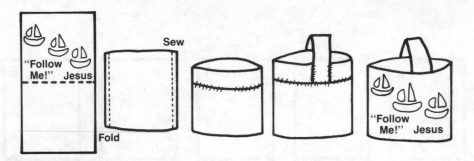

Tote Bag

Cut white trigger cloth or canvas 11″ x 20″.

Make pattern on stencil paper or poster board. Place fabric on fabric paint hoop or pad of newspaper. Tape in place.

Dip round stiff stencil brush in fabric paint. Wipe off excess paint on paper towel. Brush in circular motion away from edge of stencil toward center of open space on fabric. Use different brush for each color.

Use black ball-point fabric paint tube for Bible verse.

Fold fabric with design facing the inside. Sew up each side and bottom. Turn top down 1″, twice to make a smooth edge. Pin flat tape in place for handle, tucking end under edge. Hem or use iron-on fabric to hold handle in place.

PUBLICITY FOR YOUR PROGRAM

Bumper Stickers

Cut clear Con-Tact or self-adhesive paper 4″ x 13″.
   Paint slogan on paper with enamel paint.
   Peel off paper backing and place on bumper.
   Use bumper stickers to advertise events.

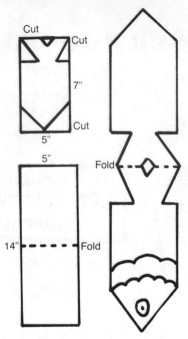

Invitations

Make invitations to come to your special programs.

Fold construction paper. Make a fish design on the front of the invitation.

Use fiber-tip pens to write a message inside.

**The King
Is Coming**

Billboards

Make billboards from poster board using fiber-tip pens.

Illustrate and announce Jesus' triumphal entry or some other Bible event. Post in various areas of the church.

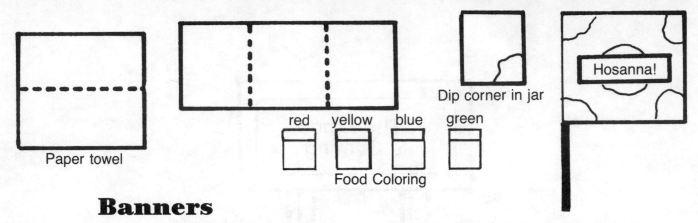

Paper towel

red yellow blue green

Food Coloring

Dip corner in jar

Hosanna!

Banners

Fold a paper towel in half. Fold again in thirds. Dip corner of folded towel in jar filled with water and a few drops of food coloring. Dip each corner in a different color.

Open towel, set aside to dry.

Write Bible verse or phrase on strips of paper, such as, "The King Is Coming," "Hosanna," "Blessed Be the King," "Glory in the Highest." Glue across face of banner.

Glue banner to wooden dowel.

Other banners may be made from felt or burlap. Cut letters from felt and glue to banner. Fasten to doweling across the top. Hang with cord.

MORE CRAFTS

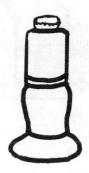

Candle Holders

Choose various sizes and shapes of jars and spools.

Use a large jar or saucer for base. Glue these jars and spools together. Place a bottle cap on top to hold candle.

Cover with a thin coat of papier-mâché. Make by tearing strips of newspaper. Then dip in thin mixture of wallpaper paste.

When dry, paint with tempera paint. Shellac when dry.

You may use gold spray paint. Work inside a cardboard box to protect surrounding area.

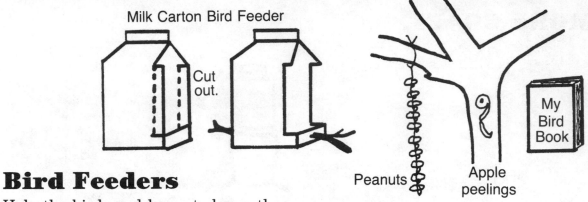

Milk Carton Bird Feeder

Cut out.

Peanuts

Apple peelings

My Bird Book

Bird Feeders

Help the birds and learn to know them.

Cut one side from a half-gallon milk carton, leaving edge on bottom. Make a hole through bottom side of carton. Insert a short branch from a tree. Place a heavy rock in the bottom of the carton. Fill with bird seed.

Tie string around each peanut, leaving enough string to tie to the branch of a tree.

Nail apple peelings to tree.

Go to the library for bird books to help you identify various birds. Keep a notebook to record data on each bird you identify. Use a separate page for each bird. Include date and place bird is seen as well as a sketch and description of bird.

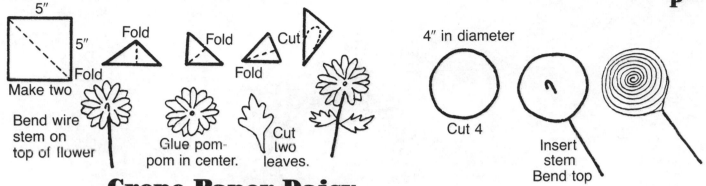

5"
5"
Fold
Make two
Fold

Fold
Fold
Fold
Cut
Fold

Bend wire stem on top of flower

Glue pom-pom in center.

Cut two leaves.

4" in diameter
Cut 4

Insert stem Bend top

Crepe Paper Daisy

Cut two 5" x 5" squares of crepe paper. Fold paper from corner to corner four times—see sketches. There will be 16 thicknesses.

Cut top in shape of petal. Open the two pieces.

Cut wire stem 8" long and insert through middle of flower. Bend stem on top of flower to hold in place.

Glue small brown pom-pom for center of flower. Tape the stem with floral tape starting with base of flower winding around stem.

Cut leaf from green crepe paper. Tape leaf to stem.

To make carnations, cut four circles 4" in diameter. Insert chenille wire through middle of flower and bend stem at top of flower to hold in place. Crush tissue paper at stem to form flower.

Daisy Chain

Make a circle with #18 gauge wire to fit head.
   Pick fresh flowers or make your own from paper.
   Use floral tape to fasten flower to wire.

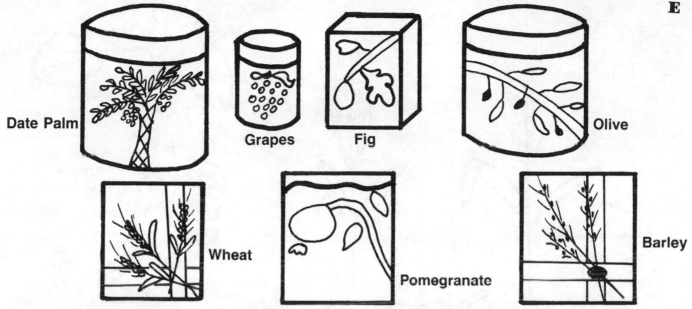

Date Palm

Grapes

Fig

Olive

Wheat

Pomegranate

Barley

Decorated Gift Cans and Boxes

Decorate oatmeal boxes or coffee cans to store candy or cookies.

Use felt, yarn, wrapping paper, metallic paper, dry materials, and greenery to cover container. Glue in place.

You may also decorate with acrylic paint—see drawings.

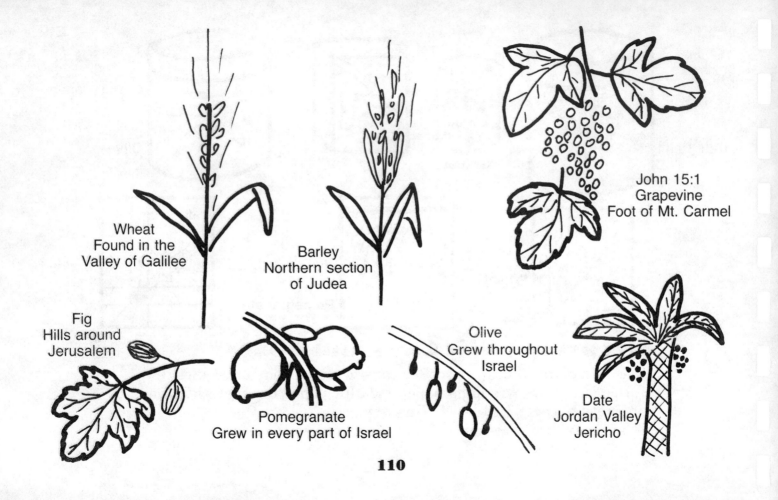

Wheat
Found in the
Valley of Galilee

Barley
Northern section
of Judea

John 15:1
Grapevine
Foot of Mt. Carmel

Fig
Hills around
Jerusalem

Pomegranate
Grew in every part of Israel

Olive
Grew throughout
Israel

Date
Jordan Valley
Jericho

110

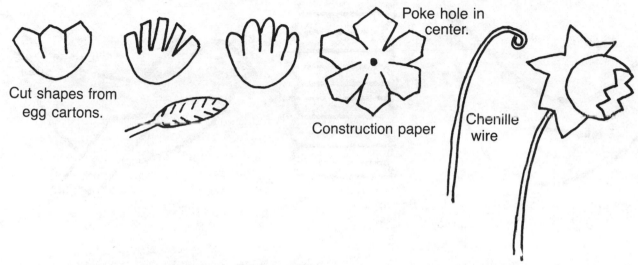

Poke hole in center.

Cut shapes from egg cartons.

Construction paper

Chenille wire

Egg Carton Flowers

Cut various shapes of flowers from pastel plastic egg cartons. Poke hole in center. Insert chenille wire stem. Curl top to hold in place.

If you wish, also cut petals from construction paper. Slip over wire. Cut leaves from egg carton or construction paper and glue to stem. Glue a small pom-pom in the center of flower.

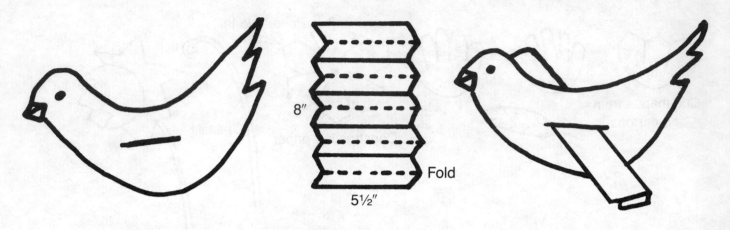

8″

5½″

Fold

Hanging Bird

Cut bird shape from construction paper. Make a slit 1″ wide horizontally across the middle.

Cut a piece of construction paper 5½″ x 8″. Fold in accordion pleats ¾″ wide. Slip through slit.

Hang bird by taping string to top.

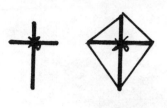 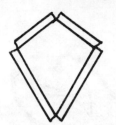 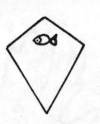  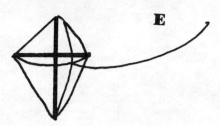

Kite

Choose two sticks—one 30″ long, the other 26″ long. Tie them together at the center.

Slit sticks at each end. Run a piece of string through the slits all the way around to form kite.

Overlay two sheets of tissue paper and glue, making paper large enough for this framework. Lay this framework on the tissue paper or waxed freezer wrapping paper.

Cut paper 1½″ larger than framework. Glue over string, folding paper back over the string and gluing in place. Cut a notch at each corner flap, permitting stick to slip through.

Decorate kite by gluing designs from colored tissue paper.

If using freezer paper, write verses such as "Be of good cheer. It is I. Be not afraid," with fiber-tip pens.

Tie string loosely from bottom to top of kite and side to side. Tie kite string to center. Tie rags on bottom of kite for tail.

113

Leaf Imprint

Roll self-hardening clay ¼″ thick with a rolling pin. Place a leaf on top of clay. Cover with a sheet of waxed paper. Press leaf with rolling pin to leave impression on clay. With a small knife, cut clay around edge of leaf.

Gently raise edges of clay leaf to give a bowl shape. Support raised edges with aluminum foil. Allow to dry.

8"

2"

Punch
holes

Measure
to fit wrist

1 yard leather string to tie wristband.

Leather Bookmark

Draw a pattern on typing paper. Cut leather to desired size. Dampen back of leather with sponge.

Place leather right side up on a smooth surface. Tape pattern to leather and trace with a modeler. (This tool for leather may be purchased at a leather craft shop.)

Remove pattern and go over the outline again. Use the spoon of the modeler to press down background to make design stand out.

Alternate idea: Punch holes and tie ends together to make a wristband.

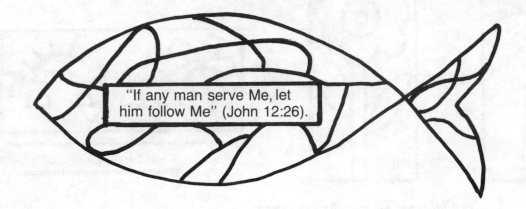

"If any man serve Me, let him follow Me" (John 12:26).

Oiled Design

On typing paper, make an outline of a picture or design with black crayon. Fill in spaces with crayon, using a variety of colors.

Dip a cotton ball in vegetable oil and rub over the back of the picture. Cut around the edge of the design. Write a Bible verse on a strip of paper and glue to design.

Cut around the edge of the design. Place over a window for a transparent effect.

Strips of newspaper

Wallpaper paste

Cover balloon

Paint and trim fish

Papier-Mâché Hanging Fish

Tear a newspaper in 1″ strips. Make a thin mixture of wallpaper paste according to directions on the package and place in a bowl. Dip strips of newspaper in paste solution.

Inflate a balloon. Wrap strips of paper around balloon until surface is completely covered. Cover with several layers of paper strips. When dry, pop balloon with a pin.

Glue several thicknesses of newspaper together with the wallpaper paste. Form fins and tail. When all parts are dry, tape together with masking tape.

Allow to dry for several days. Paint with tempera paint. Shellac. Trim with colored string and yarn.

Tie a string to top and hang from ceiling.

Makes an attractive room decoration.

117

P

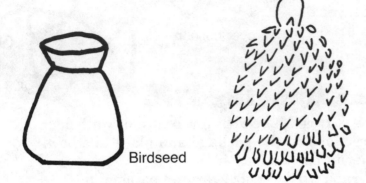
Birdseed

Peanut Butter

Pinecone Bird Feeder

Choose a large pinecone. Stuff open spaces in the pinecone with peanut butter.

Place birdseed on waxed paper. Roll pinecone in birdseed.

Tie string around top of pinecone. Fasten it to the branches of a tree.

Placemats

Cut fabric (preshrunk unbleached muslin, Indianhead, or burlap) 20″ x 14″.

Pull threads for one inch fringe around the edge. Stitch to hold edges.

Place fabric on a mat of newspaper. Pin palm branch to fabric. (Other objects can be used.) Cut out letters and pin in place. Be sure to place pins with heads inside the shape so the pins will not show on the design.

Work in a cardboard box to protect work area.

Hold aerosol paint can about a foot away from project. Spray paint. When dry, remove letters and palm branch.

119

Pomander Ball

Poke stems of cloves into skin of a medium-sized orange until the orange is completely covered. Fill a plastic bag with powdered cinnamon.

Place the clove-covered orange in the plastic bag. Shake cinnamon around orange. Remove from bag.

Fasten a ribbon around the orange with a small piece of wire. Add a bow. Slip over a coat hanger and place in closet.

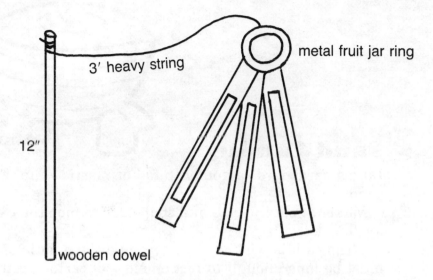

3′ heavy string

metal fruit jar ring

12″

wooden dowel

Ring Toss

Tie 3′ heavy string to a wooden dowel. Fasten a metal fruit jar ring to other end of string. Tape two or three 12″ strips of crepe paper to ring. Write Bible verses on white strips of paper and glue to streamers.

Hold dowel upright. Try to toss ring over dowel.

Sand Candle

Line a cardboard carton with foil or plastic wrap. Fill with damp sand.

Make a hole the size and shape desired for the candle. Poke holes for four large legs.

Wrap candle wick or string around the middle of a stick. (Stick must be long enough to rest on sides of carton.) Attach a nail to one end of string. Poke nail into sand to hold wick straight.

Melt wax in a can placed in a pan of water. (Be sure to follow this procedure as wax is very flammable.) Add crayons for color.

Pour melted wax into sand. If you wish different colored layers, allow each layer to cool before changing color.

When wax has hardened, dig candle from sand, allowing a thin layer of sand to remain on candle.

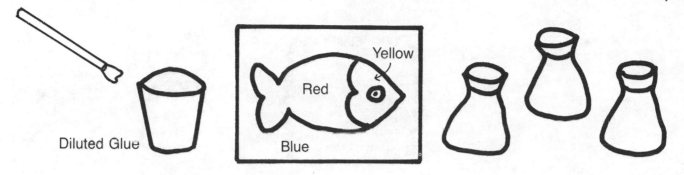

Sand Painting

Choose a simple two- or three-color design.

Outline design on construction paper.

Mix one part dry tempera paint with four parts white sand in plastic bag.

Paint an area of the design with diluted glue—one part water to one part white glue.

Use teaspoon to sprinkle area with one color of sand. Allow to dry. Shake off excess sand.

Repeat this procedure with each additional color.

E

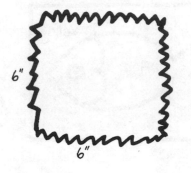

Spice Swag

Cut six strands of macrame cord three yards long. Fold in half. Tie a knot at the top. Braid in flat braid. Tie a knot at the bottom, allowing fringe to hang down.

Mix powdered cinnamon, ground cloves, and ground allspice.

Cut a square of gingham or calico fabric 6″ x 6″. Place spices in center of fabric. Pull edges together. Tie with colored yarn. Fasten several bags to macrame swag with yarn.

String Art

Cut decorative shapes from colored cardboard. Choose colorful string, yarn, pom-poms, and tassels.

Place white glue on surface of cardboard. Wind string or yarn on glue for design.

Make a loop at top for hanging. Attach a Bible verse. String art makes fine gifts.

P

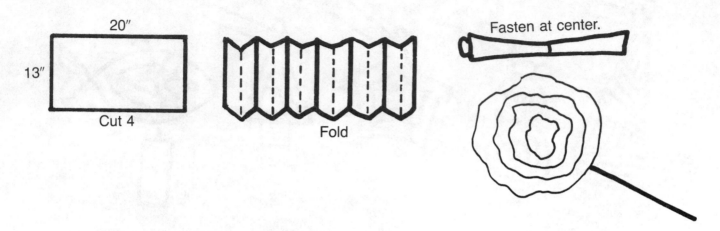

20"

13"

Cut 4

Fold

Fasten at center.

Tissue Paper Flowers

Cut four pieces of tissue paper. Fold in accordion pleats. Fasten tightly at the center with a rubber band.

Pull tissue loosely from end to end to form flower. Stick dowel through the rubber band on back to form stem.

A flower may also be made from a cleansing tissue. Fasten at middle with chenille wire.

Flowers, leaves, fern

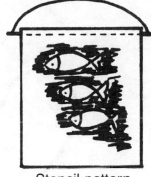

Stencil pattern

Wall Hanging

Use tape with adhesive on both sides to press flowers, leaves, and ferns onto burlap, muslin or Indianhead. You may also make a paper stencil.

Dip round, stiff stencil brush in fabric paint. Wipe off excess paint on a paper towel. Brush paint away from stencil.

When paint is dry, remove pattern or objects. Hem across top of the hanging, turning the edge under. Insert dowel. Fasten cord at both ends of dowel.

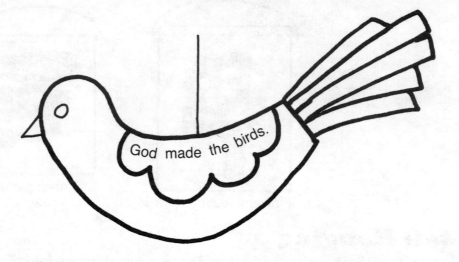

God made the birds.

Whirly Bird

Cut two birds from construction paper. Glue different colored paper for wings, eyes, and beak on one bird.

Trim the tail with strips of colored paper or feathers. Tape string to bird.

Back the first bird with the second bird. Place a paper clip on the bird's beak for balance. Hang from ceiling.

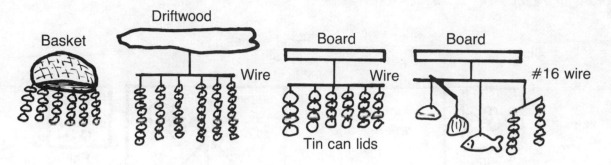

Basket — Driftwood — Board — Wire — Board — Wire — Tin can lids — #16 wire

Wind Chimes

Collect seashells. Place a shell on a board. With a small nail, gently hammer hole in shell. Experiment with shells of different sizes.

String shells on nylon fishing string, tying a knot after stringing each shell.

Hang strings of shells from driftwood, a basket, or #16 gauge wire, making a mobile.

You may hang other objects, such as a tin can lid. For a colorful effect, glue tissue paper over these objects.

GROWING THINGS

The Four Seasons

Take a walk to observe and obtain specimens found during each specific season. Ask the question, "What did you see when you took a walk?" Record observations. Illustrate.

Make folders for spring, summer, fall, and winter using manila folders. Mark seasons on cover.

Growing plants

Day	1	2	3	4	5	6	7	8	9	10	11	12
	✓	✓	✓	✓	✓	✓	Seeds Sprouted	1″	2″			

Sponge Garden

Place sponge in a small bowl filled with water. Sprinkle grass seed on top of the sponge. Keep sponge damp. Check daily. Record data. Measure growth with ruler and record.

"Awake, O north wind; and come, thou south; blow upon my garden, that the spices thereof may flow out" (Song of Solomon 4:16).

Carrot Top Plant

Cut off about ½″ of the top of a carrot. Remove any of the green top. Place the carrot in a bowl filled with small pebbles and water. In a few days a tiny plant should begin to sprout.

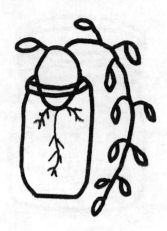

Sweet Potato Vine

Place the sweet potato in a jar holding it in place with toothpicks. Add enough water in the jar to submerge about ⅓ of the potato. The pointed end should be down. Place it in the sunlight. Add water as needed.

Jesus said, "I am the true vine, and My Father is the husbandman" (John 15:1).

How Seeds Grow

Place blotter paper or heavy construction paper around the inside edge of a jar. Fill the inside with loose soil or sand. Poke seeds between blotter and glass. Pour enough water into jar to moisten the paper. Place in a sunny area. Keep moist.

How to Preserve Leaves

    1 pint glycerin
    2 pints water
    Branch of fall leaves

In a gallon jar, mix one pint of glycerin and two pints of water.

    Crush the end of the stem of a branch of brightly colored leaves. Place stem of branch in the solution. Leave for two weeks.

    Remove branch and use in decorations. Talk about how God has made the seasons.

Sunflower in a Carton

Obtain a five-gallon container. Mix one part potting soil to one part sand. Fill carton.

Plant two or three sunflower seeds about ½" deep. Seeds will sprout in about two weeks.

Water whenever dry. As flower grows, increase water.

When flower turns brown, cut off head and hang in a dry, cool place. Remove dried seeds and soak them in salt water overnight. Drain and spread on a cookie sheet.

Bake at 200 degrees for one and one half hours.

PUPPETS

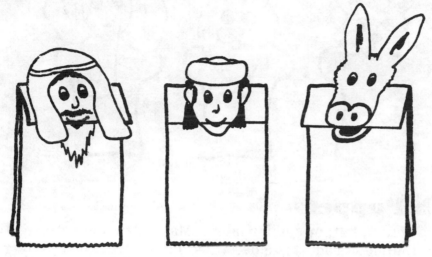

Bag Puppets

Cut faces from construction paper. Glue top part of face to bottom of a flat bag. Glue lower part of face to side of bag.

Trim with yarn, fabric, or cotton batting. Use puppets to play out Bible stories.

Cloth Puppets

Purchase denim, felt, or similar fabric. Make a simple pattern. Top will be a rounded head—to be decorated later. Cut two of pattern from fabric.

Sew around entire edge except the bottom. Stuff head with cotton batting. You may paint or stitch a face. Add yarn hair, felt ears, buttons, or decorate in any way you like.

Slip hand in bottom of puppet. Insert one finger in head and a finger in each arm (or paw). Children will enjoy moving the puppets and talking for them.

Glove Puppets

Glue yarn pom-poms on fingers of white work gloves. Trim with yarn and felt. You may be able to purchase eyes at a craft store.

Insert hand into glove. Work individual fingers as you tell the story.

Paper Plate Puppets

Use two paper plates for each puppet. Draw face on one plate. You
may use yarn for hair or draw the hair on both plates. Trim as you
like.

Staple around the edge of the two plates as they are back to back.
Leave an opening at the bottom for hand to move puppet.

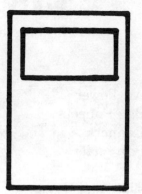

Puppet Theater

Stick Puppets

Cut cardboard shapes in duplicate. You may also use faces from pictures, making a backing to fit.

Insert tongue depressor between shapes and glue. Decorate with crayons and fiber-tip pens.

You may make a theater for your stick puppets from a shoe box. Cut an opening in the lid. Tape the lid to the box. Cut out the bottom of the shoe box and let puppets appear before the opening.

ALPHABETICAL
LISTING OF ACTIVITIES

P = Preschool children   E = Elementary school children

P	Air Power	39
P, E	Bag Puppets	137
P, E	Banners	104
E	Barometer	47
P, E	Baskets	57
E	Bibleland Game	63
E	Bible Verse Scramble	77
E	Bible Verse Village	78
P, E	Billboards	103
P	Bird Feeders	106
P, E	Boats Galore	48
P, E	Bumper Stickers	101
E	Candle Holders	105
E	Capernaum News	49
P, E	Carrot Top Plant	132
E	Cast Net Collage	26
P	Circle Board	69
E	City of Jerusalem	79
P, E	Cloth Puppets	138
E	Clothespin/Chenille Wire Figures	50
P	Collage	20
P	Crayon Resist	58
P	Crayon Rubbings	40
P	Crepe Paper Daisy	107
P	Crepe Paper Relief	70
E	Cross-stitch	88
P	Daisy Chain	108
E	Decorated Boxes	109
E	Designer T-shirt	27
E	Diorama of Capernaum	41
P	Egg Carton Flowers	111
E	Felt Board	89
E	Fish	28
E	Fish Cushion	90
E	Fish Game	91
E	Fish in Nets	29
P	Fish Mosaic	21
E	Flying Fish Kite	30
P	Folding Book	86
P, E	Four Seasons	130
E	Gifts from God's Creation	80
P	Gifts from God's Wonders	42
E	Glove Puppets	139